D0594855

withdrawn

PITCH PERFECT:

How to Write a Successful College Admission Essay

MOLLY MOYNAHAN

Foreword and Illustrations

by Jennifer Rapp Peterson

Published with:

indie**made**press.com

Text Copyright © 2012 Molly Moynahan

Illustrations Copyright © 2012 Teetersaw, Inc.

All rights reserved.

ISBN: 1467926485
ISBN-13: 978-1467926485

DEDICATION

To all teenagers bound for college and their amazing stories.

TABLE OF CONTENTS

FOREWORD

by Jennifer Rapp Peterson

When I graduated from high school, I didn't know how to write. I mean, I could spell words and push them together in a grammatically correct manner, but I certainly didn't understand how to write an essay.

I never knew that I could offer my REAL opinion, or inject some of my personality into my work and write about how I related to the subject.   I understood myself very little as a high school student. I only thought about how to get by and how to give my teachers what I thought they wanted.

Early in college, I read an essay by a good friend of mine, who was an A student and an English major. As I read, I thought, "this is all about what she thinks! ....WOW, I could never do *that*." Somehow, my junior year I finally had the courage to take a creative writing class. We sat in a circle and shared our writing – some really bad and some really good.

This class *freed me*. I learned to write creatively. I then learned to *love* writing. Especially when I could tell readers what I thought. Persuasion rocks! I changed my major and graduated with a BA in English 2 years later.

GO CRAZY

This book will teach you how to articulate what you are feeling about anything and everything — including how you feel about getting into the college of your dreams. The writing exercises will help you cultivate a relationship with yourself. This book is *all about you*!

Writing the "perfect pitch" essay requires you to think a little about who you are, where you've been, what you want and how life affects you. This book will ask you to dig deep and sift through the debris. Creative writing has a way of uncovering memories, dreams, ideas and other stuff that has been lying dormant in you. It helps give perspective and meaning to some of your experiences.

You have complete permission to go *c r a z y* with the creative writing prompts. You can even be a potty mouth in your journal. In fact, I encourage you to write imperfectly. Do not edit yourself here. Some of your writing will suck. But you have to do the bad writing to get to the good stuff. And later, somewhere, between the lines of what you write, you will find your creative, authentic voice. This voice is unique. Only you can access it.

Colleges and Universities want to hear from the authentic you. They actually want to know what you think. They want thinkers going to their school. Imagine that.

ON TOPIC

The second part of the book speaks to choosing your topic. After you have done some creative writing, you should have better insight into focusing on a subject. Your application essay needs to be great whether it's one of the Common Application prompts or a prompt unique to a certain University. Once you start working with the exercises in this book, everything you write will begin to resonate with heart and thoughtfulness.

Not only do you need to find a worthwhile topic, you must make it a worthwhile read for those reading your essay. Who is this audience? How will you make this A) understandable and B) interesting? When I work, I pretend I am explaining my thoughts to someone unfamiliar and uninterested in my topic. The *who, what, where, when, how* are nice, but *why*?

GET HEARD

You will want to pay close attention to the last part of the book, which has insightful, practical direction to edit and polish your words while keeping your authentic voice.

Editing and polishing gets you *heard.* It makes your voice accessible to others. Editing is an art form unto its own.

For me, learning to write well and authentically totally changed my life. I have launched successful careers and businesses based on my unique voice and how well I communicate it.

Communicating well gets you taken seriously. It moves people to act.

Once you access and hone your authentic voice for your college admission essay, just think about what writing well will do for your grades — not to mention the rest of your life.

My advice: read this book and work its magic to open the doors of the college of your dreams, and beyond.

AUTHOR'S NOTE

Dear Applicant:

Yes, you are much more than an applicant but that is who you are to your chosen college until you tell the admission committee something memorable in a way that convinces them that you will bring something unique and powerful to their freshman class. (By the way, your sentences should be shorter then this!) And try not to bore or depress the reader. They are bored and depressed already.

Get a notebook and a pen. Okay, a pencil if you insist but I can't get excited about something written in pencil. Make sure the notebook has lines the right width apart. Yes, you can use an iPad or your computer but a paper notebook is fail safe and let's face it, easy, not to mention portable.

Seriously, there is no magic formula for writing an excellent college admission essay. But there are certain exercises and habits that you can try, which will provide great material. This material, your life, your experiences, your discoveries and your setbacks will be the ingredients for the stunning creation you construct by blending, combining, omitting, and folding in your own secret spices. (By the way, the previous metaphor is okay, not great.) Also, everything in this book will make you a better writer, period. If you decide to take a year off to learn to juggle or travel to faraway places or you apprentice to become a welder or a mechanic or a chef, you will still benefit enormously from using this book to guide you as a writer.

Your essay should not repeat what has been learned about you through your transcripts. Awards, perfect grades, a myriad of extra-curricular activities are wonderful but the essay should take that flat, bland perfect and add the shading, the dimensions, the secret self that causes a reader to nudge his colleague and read what you have written aloud. This is what I like to refer to as "pitch perfect," writing that comes from the authentic you. Your story doesn't have to be tragic or hard to believe. Just tell something worth hearing, to engage, engross and possibly provoke.

In the BEGINNING section of this book we will focus on writing exercises that help reveal who you are. Keep a journal and start witnessing your own life. What are you thinking about? Read the newspaper online or a hard copy, pay attention to your family and friends, write down memorable quotes, read as many books as possible, write about books, movies, songs, poems that make you go *huh?* If you are out in nature and moved by something, figure out what that something is. Are you a water person, a cloud lover, a mountain climber, a snow bunny, a desert fan?

Describe what you feel, see, taste, touch, smell. Be as concrete and specific as possible. Pay attention!

I used to love T.S. Eliot, Sylvia Plath and Joni Mitchell. Yes, I was a morbid girl full of longing for things that would probably ruin my life. But I kept a journal and those lines from the past have proven useful to me as a writer. There will be much to ignore in your journal but think how powerful it will be to quote yourself rather than those overused Thoreau or Emerson adages! Your words are better than even Lady GaGa's (avoid!) or CeCe Low or _____.   Fill in the blank.

In the MIDDLE part of this book we will look to extending these shorter exercises, show you how to write a powerful persuasive essay that could easily be the element that causes your application to rise above the others, your voice and personality intact in a well-crafted essay. We will focus on prompts and how to answer them, how to use those answers to inspire story — your story — a story that a reader finds compelling, authentic and effective. You will understand the importance of audience, of conflict and resolution, and of leaving the reader with something powerful to mull.

In the END section of this book you will learn how to edit your essay, how to proofread and polish, how to hone and distill your writing into something you feel proud to have created, a piece of writing you can own without having to label it my college admission essay. Someday when you are old you will reread this document and be surprised and pleased at the depth of your thoughts, the excellence of your writing and the magic of an essay that perfectly represents who you are now. So, let's get started!

Molly Moynahan

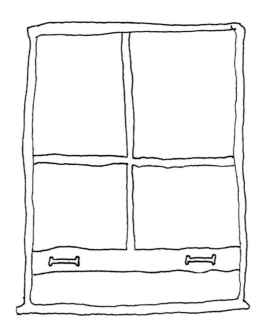

BEGINNING

"Whatever you can do, or dream you can do, begin it;
boldness has genius, power and magic in it."
~ Johann Wolfgang von Goethe

Sometimes a first sentence opens the door so the other words follow in a nice straight line, well-behaved and perfectly spaced. Sometimes. Other times a first sentence mocks, jeers and eludes. What to do?

- Begin in the middle
- Write the ending first
- Go with anything that gets you into your essay remembering this is ROUGH
- Type Blah, blah, blah and then go on
- Pull a quote from a book, a lyric, a movie and use it to start. It may or may not survive your essay but it will get you started

Think about the "wake up call" - your beginning can/should shock, stun and intrigue your reader. Get into the action immediately so the reader is wondering, "What's happening next?"

Remember, your goal is to finish the marathon, not stop in the first mile!

You don't have to be great to get started, but you have to get started to be great.

~Les Brown

It is better to write a bad first draft than to write no first draft at all.

~Will Shetterly

You only learn to be a better writer by actually writing.

~Doris Lessing

The idea is to get the pencil moving quickly...Once you've got some words looking back at you, you can take two or three - throw them away and look for others.

~Bernard Malamud

If my doctor told me I had only six minutes to live, I wouldn't brood. I'd type a little faster.

~Isaac Asimov

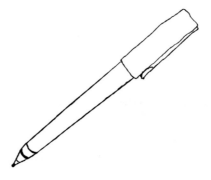

These pens indicate writing exercises or tasks.

Welcome to Creative Boot Camp. The first set of exercises in this book (#1 - #4) are designed to tighten, stretch and strengthen your writing muscles! Do one of these weekly.

Keep a file on your computer or a section of your notebook to track your progress.

Your essay will come from an excess of material, from tons of possibilities and lots and lots of writing!

MOYNAHAN

1. Show & Tell (Remember Show & Tell?)

For your writing assignment, choose something for **show & tell**, but rather than bringing your object to class, your job is to write a short story or poem that shows us the object and tells us why it's important to you.

You'll need to use lots of details to demonstrate the significance of the object — use your words to create images that *show* readers the object and why it is important to you. Open that box that contains shells you collected, toys, ticket stubs, cards or notes, any artifact that comes with a story. You can start with "I remember" or by describing the object in detail.

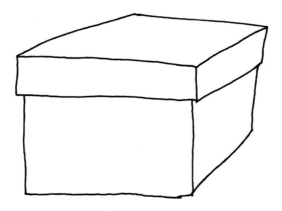

2. The Prix-Fixe Menu

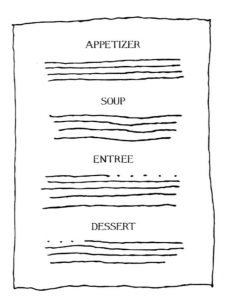

Here we have four choices — character, setting, time and situation. Choose one from each category and write a short essay that conveys something significant about YOU. Try for writing one of these a week. Throw some drawings in here if you are a visual artist. Feel free to write this in the form of a poem or a monologue. Think about how to create the perfect combination, the perfect feast, the perfect essay. Rules can be broken here, just go deep!

Choose one from each list and write!

Character

- a new mother

- a photographer

- a recent high school graduate

- a restaurant owner or manager

- an alien from outer space

- a homeless child

- a 93-year-old woman

- an environmentalist

- a college student

- a jazz musician

- your choice

Setting

- A train or bus (public transport)

- a wedding reception

- a celebration party

- an expensive restaurant

- a shopping mall

- a city park

- the porch of an old farmhouse
- a large body of water
- a college library
- a concert hall
- your choice

Time

- during a forest fire
- after a fight
- the night of high school graduation
- after a big meal
- sometime in December
- late at night
- after a big thunderstorm has passed
- in early spring
- first week of the school year
- during a concert
- your choice

Situation/Challenge

- an important decision needs to be made
- a secret needs to be confessed to someone else

- someone's pride has been injured

- a death has occurred

- someone has found or lost something

- someone has accused someone else of doing something wrong

- reminiscing on how things have changed

- someone feels like giving up

- something embarrassing has just happened

- someone has just reached an important goal

- your choice

3. Scavenger Hunt

Step One:

For the next week, you're on a scavenger hunt. Usually, when you have a scavenger hunt, you physically gather objects on a list. Instead of gathering the objects on your list, write complete descriptions of the items as you find them. Or take a picture with your cell phone and write what you saw or heard later.

- unexpected beauty

- an angry exchange

- something unpleasant

- an out-of-place object

- something fresh, new, or unused

- a well-loved object

- a lost or forgotten object

- something well-used

- a home-made or hand-made object

Step Two:

Write a story incorporating at least half of the descriptions that you found in your scavenger hunt. Weave in details, words, and phrases from your descriptions, but be discriminating — use the details, words, and phrases that fit well and help your story. Focus on revealing WHO YOU ARE without telling. Rewrite and revise the original descriptions as necessary. Feel free to break them up, rearrange them, or add more information.

Now, focus on ONE of the items from your scavenger hunt and use it to write a story about yourself. For example, let's say you opened a drawer you've opened 100 times but this time you see that pen you were given and believed lost. A pen that had promised to help you write great lyrics. Tell the reader about this moment...

4. Random Words Epigraph*

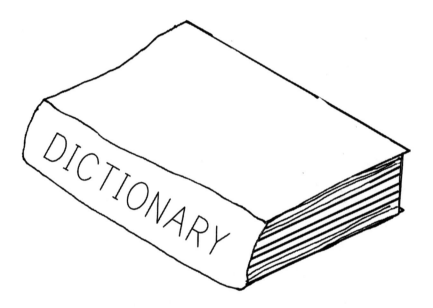

* Epigraph – an epigraph is a phrase, quotation, or poem that is set at the beginning of a piece of writing to suggest its theme.

Step One:

Randomly choose 15 entries from your dictionary. Just flip through the pages, close your eyes, and put your finger down on the page. Copy down the word that is closest to your finger. If your finger lands on a word that you don't know, you can choose the word just above or just below it. For the purposes of this assignment, count paired words as a single entry (for instance, melting pot is listed as a single entry).

Step Two:

Shape your list of dictionary entries into a poem, using at least ten of the entries (you can, of course, use them all if you want). You can add articles, helping and to be verbs, coordinating conjunctions, and prepositions.

Step Three:

Use your poem as an epigraph for an essay. Compose an essay that incorporates the themes and images that are included in your poem. The relationship between the poem and your essay should be clear to your readers, but it should not be stated explicitly in your essay. Your job is to use the poem as a jumping off point. You can add more images and themes, but those that are included in your poem should reflect the major images and themes in your story.

5. Place Poem

To write a place poem, choose a place that you remember well and want to share with others. This poem relies on your filling in a form. If you're unsure of the parts of speech, check your grammar handbook.

Here's the format:

What's Needed	Example
3 adjectives	cool, quick, smooth
An abstract noun	beauty or truth
A participial phrase	flowing swiftly downward
A prepositional phrase	over the edges of reality
2 participial phrases	defying sense
The place name	Niagara Falls

You can format your poem any way that you like. Use more punctuation or less. Change the line breaks. Align the words with the margin. Use capital letters, play with the arrangement of the words on the page, and so forth. Be creative!

Note: Places can reveal much about a person. I am an ocean person, which suggests a certain amount of lawlessness and love of movement. I don't like being contained.

6. Six Word Personal Essay

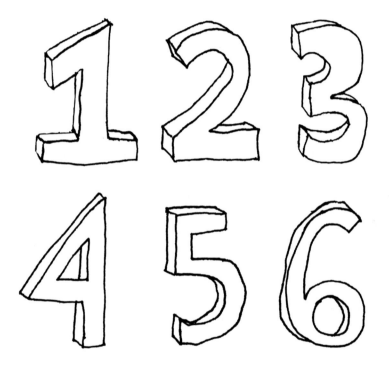

Writing the college essay requires the powerful use of words, words to describe who you are. If you only present your perfect self, the self you trot out when you are interviewed for a job or talking to an authority figure, the whole imperfect, exciting individual that you are, may be lost.

Without editing: SIX POWER WORDS a friend would use to describe you.

1.

2.

3.

4.

5.

6.

Without editing: SIX POWER WORDS a sibling, a teacher, a friend would use to describe you, *after a dispute.*

1.

2.

3.

4.

5.

6.

With editing: SIX POWER WORDS to describe you to an employer or a professor.

1.

2.

3.

4.

5.

6.

Take the best of these 18 words and write a paragraph to introduce yourself. Your goal is to make a positive impression but to also be perceived as well rounded and real. Your audience is someone who really wants to know you but also needs to choose you from a large group of other candidates. A suggestion: Print out these 6 words and put them where you can see them every day. Use them as inspiration. If they don't inspire you, find six new words!

Notes:

7. How to Keep a Journal

I know. It's the bane of many writers' existence — the stupid journal that records the painful process by which we inch through life. My early journals were mainly whining about boys, my hair, my weight, school, my parents and, occasionally, something I considered unjust, some societal ill that suddenly attracted my scrutiny: war, racism, poverty or sexism.

However, my journals have fed my writing in a number of ways.

- **Keeping a record**
- **Capturing a moment**
- **Pure writing practice**
- **A memorable phrase or sentence**

Many of us aren't sure what we should be writing about during that space we set up for writing every day. At first we might have a good idea for a poem, or a few phrases that could fit into a song, or maybe an interesting conversation that could be part of a story, novel, or play. But the next day, or the day after, we don't have any ideas. What should we do then? This is where keeping a journal comes in.

A journal can be physically made of anything that it is convenient for you to write in and carry around. You'll have to discover what works best for you – loose leaf, sewn, ring binder, a file on your laptop, something that fits easily into your back pocket – whatever. The idea is that you have something to write in every day and that you can keep it handy.

You use a journal in two basic ways: as a place for writing every day and as a resource to jot down ideas, images, phrases and descriptions as you encounter them. Pictures ripped from magazines or photos taken on your phone can be placed in your folder also. The journal becomes a ready reference, a source book for later writing projects, including having something to write about during that time you set aside to write.

Ways to Fill Page One

There is no right or wrong way to begin a journal, just as there is no right or wrong way to maintain one. Take a deep breath and begin writing. Here are a few ideas to get your pen moving:

Sankalpa

This is the Sanskrit word for intention. Give your journal an intention. Start at the top of the page and you can choose a different intention each time you write. If you are angry you can make your intention understanding that anger or possibly just expressing it. Try to avoid a wholly negative intention. Date your intentions and see if a pattern forms. Are you frequently seeking peace, inspiration, and calm?

Dedication

Many books begin with a dedication page. You can dedicate your journal to a person, a place, a thing (skateboard, iPod) or maybe a band or an idea. This is your book so you get to choose.

Art

Draw, practice impressive looking signatures, make a collage, paste in ticket stubs, dried flowers, anything that defines who you are: a photograph of you, your cat, your dad, your neighbor!

Your Motto or Mission Statement

Take a cue from successful businesses, and craft a personal mission statement or a motto. Where I grew up the city of Trenton had the motto *Trenton makes, the world takes.* Do you live to make people laugh? Are you unflinchingly honest? Are you on a quest to improve the environment, bake the perfect loaf of bread, do a perfect kick flip on a skateboard? Write a mission statement that expresses your goal.

Stolen Lines

Write down lines from poems, movies, something one of your friends said, a quote you love, a lyric you can't shake.

Letters

Write a letter to yourself in five years.

Current Events

Take some time to capture the events that are shaping history. What is going on in your city, your country, or the world? What are your thoughts and opinions about these events?

Lists

Make a list – your favorite books, movies, bands, foods, places, colors...whatever.

Three Wishes

Okay, you rubbed the lamp and the genie appeared. What will you ask for?

Introduction

Pretend you are someone else and introduce yourself. Be your dog, your best friend, that weird kid in your math class.

> *Man can starve from a lack of self-realization as much as...*
> *from a lack of bread.*
> **~Richard Wright, *Native Son*, 1940**

> *No one remains quite what he was when he recognizes*
> *himself.*
> **~Thomas Mann**

> *Every one of us has in him a continent of undiscovered*
> *character. Blessed is he who acts the Columbus to his own*
> *soul.*
> **~Author Unknown**

> *He who knows others is learned; He who knows himself is*
> *wise.*
> **~Lao-tzu, Tao te Ching**

All men should strive to learn before they die what they are running from, and to, and why.

~**James Thurber**

I know well what I am fleeing from but not what I am in search of.

~**Michel de Montaigne**

There is nothing like returning to a place that remains unchanged to find the ways in which you yourself have altered.

~**Nelson Mandela**

The indispensable first step to getting the things you want out of life is this: decide what you want.

~**Ben Stein**

Those who are brutally honest are seldom so with themselves.

~**Mignon McLaughlin, *The Second Neurotic's Notebook*, 1966**

Your work is to discover your world and then with all your heart give yourself to it.

~Buddha

There is an eternal landscape, a geography of the soul; we search for its outlines all our lives.

~Josephine Hart

The simplest questions are the most profound. Where were you born? Where is your home? Where are you going? What are you doing? Think about these once in a while and watch your answers change.

~Richard Bach

Notes:

8. Personal Narratives (More on Journals)

Keeping a record — writing down your feelings, thoughts and ideas — is a way to document how you change and mature during the four years you attend high school. You can keep this journal on your computer or iPad or you could be really old school and purchase a big, fat college lined spiral-bound notebook!

Remember, not only are you expected to produce a memorable, interesting, honest, well-crafted college essay in the fall of your senior year, but both the ACT and SAT exams want you to write an impromptu essay based on a response to a prompt. You need to have a writing practice, a daily (or weekly) paragraph that helps you check in with how you are handling your life.

Use these topics as a guide for metacognition, which is just a fancy way to describe thinking about how you are thinking. How are you thinking? High School is a transition into the adult world. You are dealing with friends, family, social situations, academics, learning to drive, learning to handle money, making decisions about sex, drugs, drinking and finding a way to express who you are today.

Try to write at least a paragraph for each of these prompts. Consider using poetry, song lyrics or pictures. This is your record of your experience in high school. Add photographs and change your font or pen color. Create something you enjoy reading. Create something memorable, funny and affecting. These elements are desirable for all your writing.   Practice and have fun.

Freshman Year

1. Who am I?
2. How do I find my place in high school?

3. Time Capsule — things that matter to me right now

4. One thing I'm going to do differently

5. Something I won't negotiate

6. My greatest fear

7. I'm most proud of _____

8. Five Secrets

Sophomore Year

1. Stuck in the Middle

2. What has changed

3. Reaching out to a freshman

4. Reaching up to a senior

5. What drives me crazy

6. Thing I miss most about childhood

7. Five Secrets

Junior Year

1. Stop asking me about college

2. It's your fault the world sucks

3. Don't tell me I'm not old enough

4. Why do I have to take responsibility

5. Being a grownup looks terrible

6. How come I'm still so…(short, flat, fat, scared etc.)

7. Five secrets

Senior Year

1. Look how much I've changed (time capsule)

2. Five things to do before graduation

3. What it means to go to college/work/apprenticeship

4. Who am I now?

5. How did I get here?

6. My Motto, my beliefs, my credo

7. Five truths

9. The Landscape of Childhood

The childhood landscape is with you forever. That street, the tree in the neighbor's yard, the long hallway in the apartment building, the store on the way home from school — these locations have been imprinted on your brain and will forever haunt your writing on some level.

This exercise can be used to help write about the past in a concrete way, to jog the memory for writing a personal essay with strong details. Sometimes we need to stop writing and use crayons and markers, stickers and construction paper to wake up the other parts of our brains.

Draw a map of the neighborhood(s) from childhood.

Use the map to write a description of the neighborhood, using specific details and stories to develop the description.

If you have lived in several (or many!) different neighborhoods, you can try the following options:

- Draw a neighborhood that somehow combines them all together
- Choose the most memorable one and draw that
- Draw (if you lived in apartments) the map in whatever format makes the most sense to you

The map should have the following content:

- Drawings of landscape details (trees, rivers, streets, parks, buildings — whatever)
- Label all the details — note special places (e.g., Place at the brook where we built dams or Place where we played baseball/tag on summer evenings)

- Symbols or images that represent events that happened. (One night our barn burned to the ground. One afternoon the horses jumped the fence. One day my sister came home on a stretcher.)

Use crayons and other art supplies to draw this map on an 8.5 x 11 sheet of blank white paper. When you finish the map describe the neighborhood in writing. Try to do the following when you write:

- Tell stories; don't just summarize the drawing
- Use descriptive language: concrete nouns, active verbs, and precise adjectives

Have fun with it! Make it look cool!

Tell a story that occurred in this place. Make sure you describe yourself in this landscape.

Notes:

10. Graphing your Life

You are going to create a graph about your life so far. On it you will put some of the high points and some of the low points. But remember, you do not have to put anything on the graph that makes you uncomfortable.

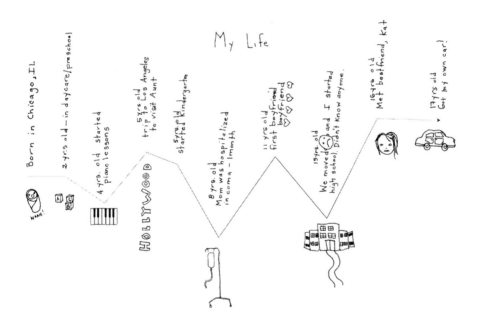

1. Across the bottom of the graph put the years.

You can use the year you were born as a beginning place, or you can use the various ages you were when the events happened. I would start at 3 when we moved to London. (1960) Then I'd go up by 5-year increments and include whatever I can remember that seems important TO ME!

2. Start by making a list of some of the things that have happened to you. Think about:

- Moves you have made—from one house to another or one school district to another
- friends you have made
- grandparents who have died
- pets
- the birth of brothers and sisters
- a time when you got hurt
- a time when you won something
- a special birthday
- a divorce in the family
- a time when you did something embarrassing
- an unexpected death in the family or in the neighborhood
- the day you fell in love with somebody
- the day you fell out of love with somebody
- something that happened to you during a sport or a game
- anything else that is meaningful to you that you want to share

3. Begin thinking about the chart or graph.

Number your paper from one to ten down the side. Ten will indicate the best things that have happened to you, one will indicate the worst things. The numbers in between will indicate how you feel about some of the events that fall in between the best and the worst.

4. Now it's time to place the events in your graph.

Put a dot when the event happened and how it rates on the best/worst scale. When you are finished, draw a line to connect the dots and you will see the graph. Add and adjust things, as you need to.

5. Final steps

Take your graph and copy it onto a clean sheet. Mark the events in your life with pictures, stickers, and colors, things that represent your progress across the years.

Choose one of these events each day and use it to inspire a page of writing. The topic does not have to be connected to college or school. Try and tell something significant about yourself but don't feel like it has to be serious.

Also, choose a side. Write persuasively using all the persuasive techniques possible. Write at least a full page.

Notes:

MIDDLE

You are a bundle of mysteries. Finding and conquering yourself is a lifetime task. There are unplumbed depths in you full of the rich ore of personal discovery. Explore yourself! There is power in you – the power to change yourself and to change the world; the power to create plans, projects, and movements for the common good; the power to inspire and serve.

~Wilfred Peterson

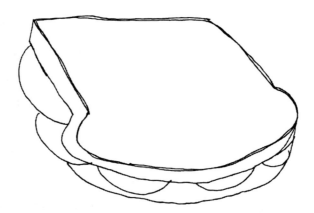

Nobody wants to be in the middle. You're the monkey, people keep squishing you, you can't say "the oldest" or "the youngest," and you are neither here nor there. Well, take advantage of this position and make it a strength! Refresh, re-imagine, reinvigorate and reinvent.

Applying to college marks a true turning point and the middle of your essay is a metaphoric crossroads. Anything can happen. Some tips to keep the energy up:

- Exercise — take a walk, swim, run, bike. Do something challenging with your body and your brain might un-stick
- Feed your art appetite — go to a museum, a movie, read some poetry or a novel or your favorite blogger
- Make some art — Paper Mache, draw a picture, embroider stuff on your jeans, dye some eggs, sew sock puppets
- Have some fun — dance with your father, drink coffee with your friends, or take someone out for ice cream
- Try a little meditation — nothing too complicated, five minutes, breathe, focus on a candle, breathe, try not to fall asleep, breathe and then jump up and down and sing
- Be silly

And then go back and write. Check your thesis statement and make sure your body paragraphs deal with every element in that statement. Look at your counter-argument. Soon, your essay will be impressively long yet concise and compressed. The final miles are under your feet and you feel energized.

> *The act of writing is an act of optimism. You would not take the trouble to do it if you felt it didn't matter.*
> **~Edward Albee**

*I write for the same reason I breathe – because if I didn't,
I would die.*
  ~Isaac Asimov

*The difference between perseverance and obstinacy is that
one comes from a strong will, and the other comes from a
strong won't.*
  ~Henry Ward Beecher

You can't try to do things; you simply must do them.
  ~Ray Bradbury

It is never too late to be what you might have been.
  ~George Elliot

*Most of the shadows of this life, are caused by standing in
one's own sunshine.*
  ~Ralph Waldo Emerson

Motivation is when your dreams put on work clothes.
  ~Benjamin Franklin

He who fears he shall suffer, already suffers what he fears.
  ~Michel de Montaigne

*In any moment of decision, the best thing you can do is the
right thing. The worst thing you can do is nothing.*
  ~Theodore Roosevelt

Being defeated is often a temporary condition. Giving up is what makes it permanent.
   ~Marilyn vos Savant

I admire anybody who has the guts to write anything at all.
   ~E. B. White

The two most engaging powers of an author are, to make new things familiar, and familiar things new.
   ~Samuel Johnson

Make it new.
   ~Ezra Pound

If you don't know it, don't write it.
   ~Darrell Schweitzer

Moving around is good for creativity: the next line of dialogue that you desperately need may well be waiting in the back of the refrigerator or half a mile along your favorite walk.
   ~Will Shetterly

Notes:

11. The Sense Memory

I adapted this exercise from an acting exercise that serves to help the actor use an intense recollection to fuel a moment on stage. For writing it can be like a prop, you remember something real that produces a significant memory that might help you identify your topic.

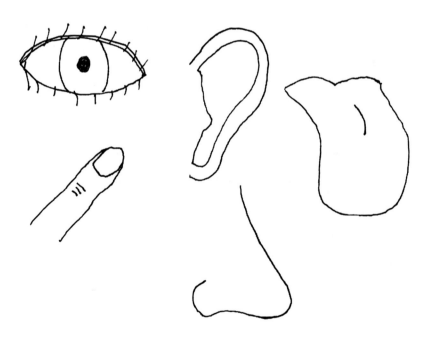

Please try for at least a full page of writing. If one object ceases to work, choose another from the list. Start with a sheet of paper in front of you so when you are ready to write, you have this handy.

Allow yourself to fully relax, close your eyes, and breathe deeply and evenly. Let your mind wander back to when you were about 7-11. Recall an inside place where you spent time, felt good and can remember at least a few details.

In your mind's eye, go there. Don't force anything. Just open the door and walk inside. Continue to stay relaxed and open. Don't criticize yourself. Turn off the negative voices. Be the person you were who might have still believed in the tooth fairy, etc.

- Start to make a mental note of all the objects in the room. Look around the floor, the walls, the ceiling, notice windows, curtains, and any details. Look for toys, etc.
- Take your pen and start making a list. You can think of this as an inventory. Just write down everything you see. If there's a color involved (green chair), make sure you include that
- When you have a full page of stuff, stop writing. Put your pen down and allow yourself to stop for a moment

- Now, go through the list and see which object or detail makes you stop and think. Circle that thing

- At the top of a fresh piece of paper, write down that object: The **"green chair"** and then start to write. You can begin with "I remember" or any way you want

- Don't talk, don't be cynical, be open, don't criticize yourself. Remember: write, imagine, and dream

Notes:

12. The Rosebud Effect

In the movie Citizen Kane the title character whispers the word, "Rosebud," as he is dying. Rosebud turns out to be the name of his beloved sled that was taken away from him as a child and burned.

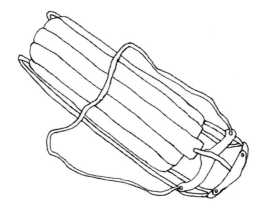

Some things are impossible to forget. What in your life has stayed with you despite intervening years or events? This thing doesn't have to be tragic or momentous.

When I was seven or eight my father's mother came to stay with us and gave everyone a present out of a small round, gray suitcase. Since it was my birthday, I was expecting something great and after the presents were distributed she gave me the suitcase. It was a pretty, girly case and I didn't have anything girly in my life. For some reason, I can never forget that moment when she handed me the case. She died the following year.

What was important in this memory?

Well, first of all, she remembered me and I was often forgotten. Second of all, she seemed to know I wanted to travel and have adventures, which meant she knew who I was. Third of all, it's the last memory I have of my grandmother.

Think of something that haunts you, something that you can't seem to forget and write about it. Be as descriptive as possible.

After you finish writing and a day or two has passed, take this writing out and reread it. Is there an element that reveals who you are without telling? Is there a powerful story attached that could lead to an essay idea?

13. The Letter (A Perfect Persuasive Document)

When I was given a Fellowship at Brooklyn College in 1988 to teach composition while I received a Masters in Fiction Writing, I found myself in a classroom full of first generation immigrants, Haitian mainly, whose writing reflected a complete disconnect between their hearts and their hands. In other words, they didn't feel connected on any level with the writing assignments I was handing out. Predictably, their essays tended to be awful, consisting of stilted, ungrammatical writing about topics they clearly didn't care about.

Filled with despair I asked them what kind of writing did they do? Who did they write for? What did they write about?

Letters, they told me, we write letters.

Of course. This was, my dears, long before the Internet, this was, in fact, years before you were born. We had typewriters but no computers. Trying to call someone in another country was a difficult, stunningly expensive undertaking. There was no electronic media.

All right, I said, we're going to write letters. Write to someone you care about very much, about something that matters to you. Make them younger.

I added the younger criteria because I wanted their essays to be very clear, very simple, and very orderly.

When they turned these essays in, I cried. Yes, your teachers are big babies. These letters were written with power and persuasion, many strong details, with clarity and authority and a clear sense of audience. And they chose topics which spoke of honor, courage, regret and love. The letter format freed them to speak with their hearts and their brains.

From now on, I told them, write me letters. Then take the *dear* and the *sincerely* away. And they did. Then they all passed the terrible writing exam the college gave in June, an exam that most of them had flunked repeatedly.

By writing these essays as letters they mastered presenting an argument, backing up that argument, and anticipating a counter-argument.

14. Persuasive Letter

Before you start this you must read Martin Luther King's Masterpiece of persuasive writing, "Letter from Birmingham Jail," and James Baldwin's love filled letter to his nephew, "Letter to my nephew on the 100th Anniversary of the Emancipation."

You can find them both on www.mollymoynahan.com.

Directions:

Use this outline to format and structure your ideas for your Persuasive Letter assignment.

You should have at least one claim and one piece of evidence for each body paragraph; however, to make your letter more effective, it may be necessary to have more than one piece of evidence for each claim.

Because each claim and its corresponding evidence equals one body paragraph, your Persuasive Letter should have at least two body paragraphs.

Topic (something you care about intensely):

Audience (someone you care about very much who is slightly younger/less experienced than you are):

1. Introductory statement

2. Claim #1

- Evidence #1
- Evidence #2

3. Claim #2

- Evidence #1
- Evidence #2

-REMEMBER THE COUNTER-ARGUMENT-

4. Concluding Statement

15. About Topics

I think it's rarely the topic but always how it is handled and whether the writer has managed to produce a piece of writing that reveals something positive and significant in a skillful manner. As a blogger I've written some pieces about predictable middle-aged woman issues — weight, work, mothering — and received positive feedback based on the emotion I expressed. Early in my career teaching high school, I worked with a student whose mother committed suicide and his essay was wonderful.

We decided as long as his essay portrayed his current emotional state as positive and healthy, the tragic part of his story would not damage his message. Mind you, I asked him to change his topic but he felt this was the story he wanted to tell. Hold tight to your truth. I was inspired by his courage and honesty and he was accepted at a very competitive University.

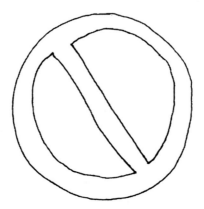

Some topics that are usually not a good idea:

- Your sex life

- How you saved someone

- Why your life is tragic

- All the great things you've already done

- All the stuff they can find elsewhere on your application

- An essay full of overused metaphors, with a cute ending, asking rhetorical questions

- Anything explicitly religious or political. You just don't know who will be reading your essay

- Anything that requires suspension of belief. Maybe you have had an amazing life full of bizarre coincidences and luck. These make great stories for your friends but often fail to translate to a thoughtful essay

- Why you hate to read/write/get up early/study
- An essay that isn't about YOU

Take your time and explore a number of possibilities. Ask people who aren't close to you to read your opening paragraph. Are they hooked? Keep going! Also, don't get too attached. I once wrote a great short story inspired by its opening sentence. On a final edit my writing teacher suggested I lose that sentence. Your story outgrew its inspiration, is what he told me. The point is, for your essay, the journey is meaningful but we will take the great story that reveals who you are any way we can!

Notes:

16. Non-Standard Prompts

Some schools have supplemental essays that might seem created to cause you pain but they want insight into you as a person and the way you think. Each prompt demands creativity and your best version of you. These prompts are less straightforward — some of them are downright weird — but at least you have a lot more flexibility in the way you can answer them.

These prompts are designed to make you slightly uncomfortable; to present an intellectual challenge that you can meet by taking a risk. If you choose the last option (pick your own prompt) in the Common Application, you might try one of these for practice.

See what repeats in your free writing and choose a topic from that element.

1) How do you feel about Tuesday?

2) You have just completed your autobiography. Write a one-page pitch of your book

3) How did you get found?

4) Write a haiku that expresses who you are

5) In the year 2050, a documentary is being made of your life. Why?

6) You are pitching a film that needs to contain the following elements. You choose the setting and the plot

   a) *A genre from the following:*

      i) Reality television

      ii) A cooking show

      iii) A documentary

      iv) A makeover show

   b) *A character from the following:*

      i) Heathcliff (Wuthering Heights)

      ii) Warren Buffet's personal trainer

      iii) A starving investment banker

      iv) A tattoo artist

   c) A prominent prop from the following:

      i) Cliff Notes for Moby Dick

      ii) Cloning Formula

      iii) Kurt Cobain's guitar

      iv) Hillary Clinton's Blackberry

17. Brainstorming Your Topic

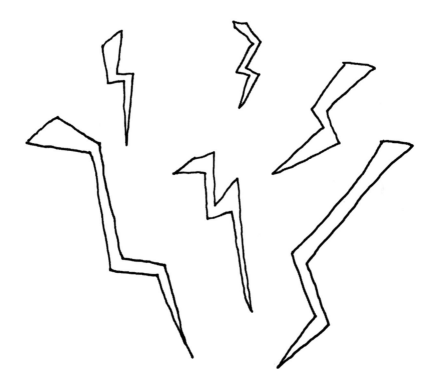

Your topic of persuasion:

- Who is your audience?

- What tone do you need to take with this particular audience? Why?

- Your angle. Your opinion

- Facts to support your position

- Personal story /examples to support your position

- What arguments will the other side make?

- How will you address and discount those arguments?

18. Rules to Remember (or Not)

In order to write, you have to hate adverbs.
~Theodore Roethke

Adverbs and intensifiers are meant to increase our writing's impact but these speech parts usually dilute the effect. The first step is easy: eliminate all intensifiers. Intensifiers are adverbs meant to strengthen other modifiers, whether adjectives or adverbs. But they rarely do. Words like very, extremely, incredibly, exceedingly, remarkably, etc. can all be eliminated because their meanings can be contained in the terms they modify. Terribly mean should be cruel. Very sad should be tragic or just sad. Extremely angry is furious.

I use the same approach on all works, whether poetry or prose: I tacitly assume that the first fifty ways I try it are going to be wrong.
~James Dickey

Start strong.

Start in the middle if you're worried about clarity. You can always return to the beginning and ground your reader in the subject. Think about how awesome movies and books begin and how you're sometimes slightly confused but still hooked. Also, accept you have no idea how to judge your own writing until you have put it aside and returned afresh.

> *Life is not a plot; it's in the details.*
> *~Jodie Picoult*

Use details but be brutal. Don't overdo the details. Constant detail is like one of those paintings with the little mouse hiding in the corner, cute but ultimately annoying.

> *Trust your heart if the seas catch fire, live by love though the stars walk backward.*
> **~E.E. Cummings**

Take risks. Be honest about yourself and how you feel.

-HOWEVER-

Numerous novels, stories, blogs even news articles contain fragments, or run-on sentences. Writing for the college essay should adhere to more formal guidelines. Each sentence should have a subject and a verb. Avoid fragments and run-ons unless you are very skilled at using them. The personal essay is safest written in Standard English. But who wants to be safe?

> *That which proves too much, proves nothing!*
> **~Anonymous proverb**

Think about pushback, also called a counter-argument. In a persuasive essay you need to consider the reader's thinking: "Yes, but...". You need to anticipate the "but" and then go ahead and let that elephant dance around your living room. You are explaining how knowing people with speech impediments has helped you see how fortunate you are to not lisp and also how the world is full of people looking for an excuse to make other people feel bad. Great.

But consider the pushback.

I had a friend who was badly brain injured in a car accident and after she came out of her coma she was a shining example of courage and tenacity. However, we once went to Manhattan and I made the mistake of leaving her to choose a flavor in a gelato store with 35 possible choices. I went to check on our car and when I returned there was a line down the block and she was trying to choose between chocolate and vanilla. I was tempted to leave her there.

This would be my push back counter-argument to my thesis about other people's struggles helping us become better human beings.

However, do not reveal your dark side. Don't admit to any behavior that is undesirable — bullying, animal torture, stealing, drug use, cheating or lying — unless it was to spare a friend — (No you don't look fat in that tube top) . Otherwise, keep that time you behaved atrociously to yourself.

-AND-

Consider your essay a chance to explain who you are, where you came from, and why it matters. No one can interrupt, distort or change this story. My son always accuses me of exaggeration and hyperbole. I am pretty sure he will keep his essay far away from me.

I laugh to keep myself from going mad.
   ~Voltaire

Be yourself.

If you are funny, write a funny essay; if you are serious, write a serious essay. Don't start reinventing yourself with the essay. If a story from your past is funny, go with it. Just make sure you have people who are funny read your essay so they can weigh in on the humor factor. Also, be careful with humor since it can be challenging to pull off in writing. Unlike a stand-up comic who can size up their live audience, you have no idea of the age, taste, background or funny bones of your readers!

> *That inner voice has both gentleness and clarity. So to get to authenticity, you really keep going down to the bone, to the honesty, and the inevitability of something.*
> **~Meredith Monk**

Don't forget your audience.

Essays should have a clear thesis. Limit the background information. Get to the story ASAP. The Common Application essay should be powerful enough to cover all the schools that accept that form but write individual essays for schools that don't or suggest a supplementary essay.

> *I was working on the proof of one of my poems all the morning, and took out a comma. In the afternoon I put it back again.*
> **~Oscar Wilde**

Proofread, proofread, and proofread.

Nothing says last-minute essay like an "are" instead of "our" or a "their" instead of "they're."

Keep it short and to the point.

Proofreadproofreadproofread

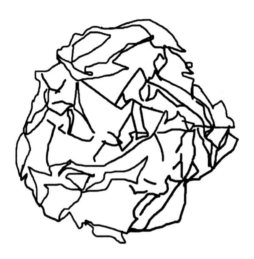

Great is the art of beginning, but greater is the art of ending.
~Henry Wadsworth Longfellow

Endings have arrived unannounced, sometimes slightly unwelcome but still, they must be allowed in. I have dreamed endings and heard someone say something that provided an ending and I have simply slapped on an ending because I was afraid to wait. Endings have also come to me like gifts, secrets whispered by angels making what came before better, leaving my readers a moment that lived beyond the page.

Some standard advice is to circle back to your opening thesis and that is a good thing to reiterate. Be sure to get all your ducks in a row as far as organization and focus. Your essay's conclusion needs to conclude. But it can also leave your readers with a question just not the question you posed in your thesis.

However, don't summarize your main points again. This may be the best place to use some emotion, PATHOS for those of you turned on by rhetoric. Look to the future! Don't leave the reader with the impression that something that happened in high school or, even worse, middle school is defining who you are now. Be positive, hopeful and optimistic even if you have experienced setbacks to reach this place of new beginnings. Your conclusion is double-edged; it finishes your essay but it is also your opening curtain.

Be brave. Write it, leave it alone, sleep on it, reread and read aloud. Find someone you can read the entire essay aloud to (not your cat or a baby) and don't make things better or different by modulating your tone. Own what is on the page and see if your ending comes logically but possibly as a nice surprise. Not a BIG surprise, a subtle one.

All writing is a process of elimination.
~**Martha Albrand**

There is no great writing, only great rewriting.
~**Justice Brandeis**

It is perfectly okay to write garbage – as long as you edit brilliantly.
~**C. J. Cherryh**

The most valuable of all talents is that of never using two words when one will do.
~**Thomas Jefferson**

Try any goddamn thing you like, no matter how boringly normal or outrageous. If it works, fine. If it doesn't, toss it. Toss it even if you love it.
~**Stephen King**

Detail makes the difference between boring and terrific writing. It's the difference between a pencil sketch and a lush oil painting. As a writer, words are your paint. Use all the colors.

~Rhys Alexander

If you start with a bang, you won't end with a whimper.

~T. S. Eliot

One of the really bad things you can do to your writing is to dress up the vocabulary, looking for long words because you're maybe a little bit ashamed of your short ones.

~Stephen King

My most important piece of advice to all you would-be writers: when you write, try to leave out all the parts readers skip.

~Elmore Leonard

Don't use words too big for the subject. Don't say 'infinitely' when you mean 'very'. Otherwise you'll have no word left when you want to talk about something really infinite.

~C. S. Lewis

Say all you have to say in the fewest possible words, or your reader will be sure to skip them; and in the plainest possible words or he will certainly misunderstand them.

~John Ruskin

Revise and revise and revise – the best thought will come after the printer has snatched away the copy.

~Michael Morahan

Use the right word and not its second cousin.

~Mark Twain

Stick to the point.

~ W. Somerset Maugham

Details make stories human, and the more human a story can be, the better.

~Ernest Hemingway

The first draft of anything is sh*t.

~Ernest Hemingway

Notes:

19. Substance

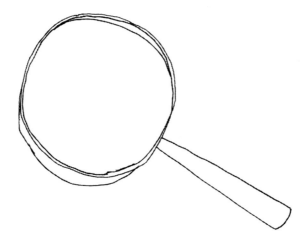

Substance refers to the content of the essay and the message you send out. It can be very hard to gauge in your own writing. One good way to make sure that you are saying what you think you are saying is to write down, briefly and in your own words, the general idea of your message. Then remove the introduction and conclusion from your essay and have an objective reader review what is left. Ask that person what he thinks is the general idea of your message. Compare the two statements to see how similar they are. This is helpful if you wrote a narrative. It will make sure that you communicate your points in the story.

Here are more questions to ask regarding content:

- Have I answered the question asked?
- Do I back up each point that I make with an example?
- Have I used concrete and personal examples?
- Have I been specific? (Go on a generalities hunt. Turn the generalities into specifics.)
- Could anyone else have written this essay?
- What does it say about me? After making a list of all the words you have used within the essay – directly and indirectly – to describe yourself, ask: Does this list accurately represent me?
- Does the writing sound like me? Is it personal and informal rather than uptight or stiff?
- Regarding the introduction, is it personal and written in my own voice? Is it too general? Can the essay get along without it?
- What about the essay makes it memorable?

20. Structure

To check the overall structure of your essay, conduct a first sentence check. Write down the first sentence of every paragraph in order. Read through them one after another and ask the following:

- Would someone who was reading only these sentences still understand exactly what I am trying to say?

- Do the first sentences express all of my main points?

- Do the thoughts flow naturally, or do they seem to skip around or come out of left field?

Now go back to your essay as a whole and ask these questions:

- Does each paragraph stick to the thought that was introduced in the first sentence?

- Does a piece of evidence support each point? How well does the evidence support the point?

- Is each paragraph roughly the same length? Stepping back and squinting at the essay, do the paragraphs look balanced on the page? (If one is significantly longer than the rest, you are probably trying to squeeze more than one thought into it.)

- Does my conclusion draw naturally from the previous paragraphs?
- Have I varied the length and structure of my sentences?

21. Interest

Many people think only of mechanics when they revise and rewrite their compositions. As we know, though, the interest factor is crucial in keeping the admissions officers reading and remembering your essay.

Look at your essay with the interest equation in mind: personal + specific = interesting.

Answer the following:

- Is the opening paragraph personal?

- Do I start with action or an image?

- Does the essay show rather than tell?

- Did I use any words that are not usually a part of my vocabulary? (If so, get rid of them.)

- Have I used the active voice whenever possible?

- Have I overused adjectives and adverbs?

- Have I eliminated clichés?

- Have I deleted redundancies?

- Does the essay sound interesting to me? (If it bores you, imagine what it will do to others.)

- Will the ending give the reader a sense of completeness?

- Does the last sentence sound like the last sentence?

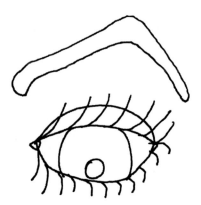

22. Proofreading

When you are satisfied with the structure and content of your essay, it is time to check for grammar, spelling, typos, and the like. You can fix obvious things right away: a misspelled or misused word, a seemingly endless sentence, or improper punctuation. Keep rewriting until your words say what you want them to say.

Ask yourself these questions:

- Did I punctuate correctly?

- Did I eliminate exclamation points (except in dialogue)?

- Did I use capitalization clearly and consistently?

- Do the subjects agree in number with the verbs?

- Did I place the periods and commas inside the quotation marks?

- Did I keep contractions to a minimum? Do apostrophes appear in the right places?

- Did I replace the name of the proper school for each new application?

- Have I caught every single typo? (You can use your spell-checker but make sure that you check and re-check every change it makes. It is a computer after all.)

Keep a list of your frequent errors — I always misspell the word *character* — and check for that alone. Some common ones: subject/verb agreement, their/there, your/you're, check those contractions carefully, check your verb tense, fragments and run-on sentences.

23. Avoid Passive Voice

The passive voice often fails to identify who or what is performing the actions you are describing. Also, the passive voice tends to result in excessive use of various forms of the verb to be, which leads to wordiness. Phrasing sentences in the active voice allows you to use active verbs that are more descriptive and that enliven your writing.

> PASSIVE VOICE: Many programs were created to put Americans back to work.

> ACTIVE VOICE: The government created many programs to put Americans back to work.

In the passive voice example, the reader does not learn who created the programs. Was it government, private corporations, or some other organization? The active voice clearly indicates where the programs originated. The passive voice robs sentences of power and weakens strong verbs. In the active voice, the subject of the sentence performs the action. In the passive voice, the subject of the sentence is the object of the action, and the actor often is unknown.

For example:

The tiger bit the zookeeper. (active)

The zookeeper was bitten by the tiger. (passive)

The zookeeper was bitten. (passive)

In the first sentence, the subject (tiger) performs the action (bit) on the object (zookeeper). In the second sentence, the subject (zookeeper) receives the action (was bitten) performed by the object of a prepositional phrase (tiger). In the third sentence, the performer of the action is unknown.

A simple rule

If somebody is doing something to somebody else, the sentence is active. If somebody is having something done to him by somebody else, the sentence is passive. If somebody is having something done to him and you don't know who's doing it, the sentence is really passive.

More reasons to avoid passive voice:

- Passive voice makes verbs less forceful
- Passive voice creates awkwardness by inverting the who-did-what-to-whom relationship
- Passive voice can sound stilted, impersonal, and falsely formal
- Passive voice can hide who or what is responsible for action – something journalists always try to avoid

There are times passive voice is justified:

- When the recipient of the action is more important than the performer of the action
- When the actor is irrelevant or unidentifiable

Notes:

_____

_____

_____

_____

_____

_____

_____

_____

_____

_____

_____

_____

_____

_____

_____

_____

_____

_____

_____

_____

_____

_____

24. Editing and Proofreading – Strategies for Revision

Once a rough draft is finished, you should try to set it aside for at least a day and come back to the essay with a fresh mind and thus more easily catch the errors in it. You'll bring a sharp eye to the process of polishing a essay and be ready to try some of the following strategies.

Read the Essay Aloud

If we read the paper aloud slowly, we have two senses — seeing *AND* hearing — working for us. Thus, what one sense misses, the other may pick up. Reading an essay aloud encourages you to read every little word. Try to read it to someone critical but supportive. (Not your mother.)

Check the Thesis Statement and Organization

Does it answer the prompt? Does it accurately state your main idea? Does the essay in fact support it? Does it need to be changed in any way? On that piece of paper, list the main idea of each paragraph under the thesis statement. Is each paragraph relevant to the thesis? Are the paragraphs in a logical sequence or order?

Remember that you are Writing for Others

No matter how familiar others may be with the material, they cannot get inside your head and understand your ideas unless you express them clearly. Therefore, it is useful to read your essay through once keeping in mind whether a reader will understand what you are saying. That is, have you said exactly what you wanted to say?

Check Your Essay's Development

Are there sufficient details? Is the logic valid?

Check the Essay's Coherence and Unity

Are the major points connected? Are the relationships between them expressed clearly? Do they all relate to the thesis?

Review your Diction

Remember that others are reading your essay and that even the choice of one word can affect their response to it. Try to anticipate their response, and choose your words accordingly.

Original: Greed and indifference caused the banking crisis.

Revision: In addition to elements like the housing bubble and the war in Iraq, many believe greed and indifference contributed to the banking crisis.

In addition to being more specific, the revision does not force the reader to agree with the writer. In the original, though, the statement is so exaggerated that the reader may feel it necessary to disagree. Thus, the writer of the original has made his job of persuading the reader that much harder.

Sentence and Word-level Issues

No matter how many times you read through an essay, you're likely to miss many of your most frequent errors. The following guide will help you proofread more effectively.

General Strategies

Begin by taking a break. Allow yourself some time between writing and proofing. Even a five-minute break is productive because it will help get some distance from what you have written. The goal is to return with a fresh eye and mind.

Try to s-l-o-w d-o-w-n as You Read Through Your Essay

It will help you catch mistakes you might otherwise overlook. As you use these strategies, remember to work slowly. If you read at a normal speed, you won't give your eyes sufficient time to spot errors.

Reading With a Cover

Sliding a blank sheet of paper down the page as you read encourages you to make a detailed, line-by-line review of the essay.

Personalize Your Proofreading

You won't be able to check for everything (and you don't have to), so you should find out what your typical problem areas are and look for each type of error individually.

Here's how:

- Find out what errors you typically make. Review instructors' comments about your writing.
- Use specific strategies. Use these strategies to find and correct your particular errors in usage and sentence structure, and spelling and punctuation.
- Check your writing for abstract subjects, particularly those you have combined with passive verbs.
- Try substituting concrete or personal subjects with active verbs.

    Original: More desirability is sometimes given an object when it is lost.

    Revision: When an object is lost, some people desire it more.

Cut out Wordiness Wherever Possible

Original: They are desirous of ...

Revision: They want ...

Avoid Using Stretcher Phrases

" It is" and "there are," are stretcher phrases; don't use them unless needed for emphasis.

Remember the need for strong verbs.

Original: There were several reasons for the "Occupy Wall Street" protests.

Revision: "Occupy Wall Street" protested for several reasons.

Replace Colloquialisms with Fresh and more Precise Statements

Because colloquialisms tend to be used so often, they also are not very precise in meaning. A hassle, for example, can be an annoyance, an argument, or a physical fight.

Original: His green hair flipped me out.

Revision: His green hair was disconcerting.

Review your Sentences . . .

Be sure that no parts of the essay are short and choppy; be sure that the rhythm of your essay is not interrupted (except for a good reason, like emphasis). A good way of smoothing out such a problem is to try combining sentences, and in so doing showing the relationship between them.

Original: "True Blood" was once the best show on television. It was always surprising. It lost its originality.

Revision: "True Blood" was once the best show on television, nearly always surprising, but lately it has lost its originality.

For Usage and Sentence Structure –

For subject/verb agreement:

1. Find the main verb in each sentence.
2. Match the verb to its subject.
3. Make sure that the subject and verb agree in number.

For pronoun reference/agreement:

1. Skim your essay, stopping at each pronoun. Look especially at it, this, they, their, and them.
2. Search for the noun that the pronoun replaces. If you can't find any noun, insert one beforehand or change the pronoun to a noun. If you can find a noun, be sure it agrees in number and person with your pronoun.

Parallel Structure

1. Skim your essay, stopping at key words that signal parallel structures. Look especially for the following: and, or, not only...but also, either... or, neither...nor, both...and.
2. Make sure that the items connected by these words (adjectives, nouns, phrases, etc.) are in the same grammatical form.

Spelling

1. Examine each word in the essay individually. Move from the end of each line back to the beginning. Pointing with a pencil helps you really see each word
2. If necessary, check a dictionary to see that each word is spelled correctly

For compound sentence commas:

1. Skim for conjunctions: and, but, for, or, nor, so and yet
2. See whether there is a complete sentence on each side of the conjunction. If so, place a comma before the conjunction

For introductory commas:

1. Skim your paper, looking only at the first two or three words of each sentence
2. Stop if one of these words is a dependent marker, a transition word, a participle, or a preposition

3. Listen for a possible break point before the main clause

4. Place a comma at the end of the introductory phrase or clause (which is before the independent clause)

For comma splices:

1. Skim the essay, stopping at every comma

2. See whether there is a complete sentence on each side of the comma. If so, add a coordinating conjunction after the comma or replace the comma with a semicolon

For fragments:

1. Look at each sentence to see whether it contains an independent clause

2. Pay special attention to sentences that begin with dependent marker words (*such as, because*) or phrases such as *for example* or *such as*

3. See if the sentence might be just a piece of the previous sentence that mistakenly got separated by a period

For run-on sentences:

4. Review each sentence to see whether it contains more than one independent clause. Start with the last sentence of your paper, and work your way back to the beginning, sentence by sentence.

5. Break the sentence into two sentences if necessary.

For left-out words:

1. Read the essay aloud, pointing to every word as you read. Don't let your eye move ahead until you spot each word.
2. Make sure that you haven't doubled any words.

Read it aloud again.

Pat yourself on the back.

And by the way, everything in life is writable about if you have the outgoing guts to do it, and the imagination to improvise. The worst enemy to creativity is self-doubt.

~Sylvia Plath

Fill your paper with the breathings of your heart.

~William Wordsworth

These master writers, Plath, who died in 1963, and Wordsworth, who died in 1850, tell the truth: writing from the heart will always trump anything formulaic or generic. Your story is as unique as your fingerprints, and you must find a way to show that identity in your essay. Be fearless and smart and thoughtful and funny if at all possible. Take a risk; reveal something about yourself that is important and significant to your future. Recognize there is much to learn and a ways to go but also note how much you have already learned and travelled.

Have you suffered and survived? Have you had a relatively smooth path? Are you someone who contemplates the future with happy anticipation or are you wondering how anything can be better than your childhood? Consider the speakers and writers that remain in your heart and memory. Who are the musicians that crafted lyrics that made you cry or fall in love? Chances are these writers succeeded in taking an ordinary situation or conflict and making it memorable with their word choices, the rhythm and pacing of their writing, the sharply chosen vocabulary and, finally, honesty and love.

Yes, good writing requires love. You must be fearless and supportive but also have high expectations. Don't settle. Wake up tomorrow and open up your file. Remove the modifiers, add a detail, recall a conversation, trust your reader, trust yourself and allow your heart to breathe.

> *Write your story, as it needs to be written. Write it honestly, and tell it as best you can. I'm not sure that there are any other rules. Not ones that matter.*
>
> **~Neil Gaiman**

Love,

Molly Moynahan

ACKNOWLEDGMENTS

Molly adores Jennifer for her brilliant art and coaching, Luke for his sweet sense of proportion and support, and the cats for being ridiculous.

Jennifer acknowledges Molly for writing this much needed manual for creative writing; Jonathan, for his patience and love during the process of putting this book together; and Ginny and Jacob, for their ceaseless creativity, love, and office visits.

ABOUT THE AUTHOR

Molly Moynahan has been writing and teaching for more than twenty years. She is a published novelist, an award-winning playwright and scriptwriter, a columnist and blogger. She teaches writing and literacy in both high school and college and currently lives in Chicago. Moynahan is the author of three novels, *Parting is All We Know of Heaven, Living in Arcadia and Stone Garden. Stone Garden* was chosen a Notable Book by the New York Times, a best teen read by the American Library Association and was a BOOKSENSE 76 choice. Moynahan has been a recipient of fellowships from the Djerassi Foundation, The Helena Wurlizer Foundation and she was a panelist at the NCTE convention in Chicago. She has finished a memoir and is currently working on a novel called The *Tug Boat's Captain's Daughter.*

ABOUT THE ILLUSTRATOR

Jennifer Rapp Peterson is an award-winning toy inventor, software consultant, irony-loving cartoonist, greeting card publisher, children's book illustrator and the founder of www.indiemade.com.

CPSIA information can be obtained at www.ICGtesting.com
Printed in the USA
LVOW041620190412

278337LV00014B/84/P